Stock Investing For Beginners

(How To Buy Your First Stock And Grow Your Money)

PLUS: Simple Ways To Pick Winners

By John Roberts

http://www.LiveLearnAndProsper.com

STOCK INVESTING FOR BEGINNERS - How To Buy Your First Stock And Grow Your Money

Copyright © 2017 by John Roberts. All rights reserved.

Published by Live Learn and Prosper, Orlando, Florida. Visit us on the web at http://www.LiveLearnAndProsper.com.

1st edition – Release 23v1 – 4/18/17. **ISBN:** 9781520876290

CONTENTS

CONTENTS

1

INTRODUCTION

A former janitor and gas station attendant in Vermont, who died a few years ago, surprised everyone by leaving an $8 million fortune to his local library and hospital.

What was his secret, everyone wondered? And the answer turned out to be pretty basic. Because, besides being industrious and frugal, which you may have guessed, *he had invested in the stock market throughout the years.*

This is actually not as surprising as it may sound. According to a recent World Wealth Report, the wealthy invest the largest part of their money into stocks and businesses. Our wise janitor had simply done what the wealthy do. So he got a similar result. That is, he grew his money into considerable wealth.

And you can do this too. Now, we aren't saying you will make $8 million. After all, this is a beginner's book and the janitor had an extraordinary result. But stock market investing is one of the best tools you can use to build a more secure financial future for you and your family.

So are you someone who wants to make money in the stock market? And does that story make you feel excited? Have you tried to understand the stock market, only to be discouraged by how complicated it all seems? And aren't you just a little bit encouraged that an ordinary person, like our janitor from Vermont, could invest in stocks and succeed?

If you answered yes to any of those questions, then this book just might be the solution you've been looking for. Because it will show you **just what you need to know, and no more, to start investing in the stock market.**

And it will describe all of this for you in simple terms you already understand. Not complicated theory. Not a mind-numbing blitz of technical buzzwords.

Just what you need to know and no more. And the few specific steps you can take to get started.

So that by the end of this book, you will be able to buy your first stock. **You will know the simple steps to grow your money in the stock market.** And start on your path to a more secure financial future.

How To Use This Book

You may be surprised that there are not that many steps to be taken. There are only seven of them. So with that in mind, here is how we will cover them.

Section 1 is what you are reading now. It's an "Introduction." Let's be realistic here. We won't shoot for a lofty goal of $8,000,000. This is just a beginner's book. But we can definitely shoot for you increasing your wealth and making money over time with your stocks.

Then in Section 2 we answer the important question, "Why Invest In Stocks?" Just like the janitor in Vermont, stocks are a very important part of your wealth strategy. They are even more important today, as many other investments, like savings accounts and bonds, pay you very little.

But stocks, over time, have consistently grown wealth. Virtually all wealthy people use them, and you should too. So we will show you why stock investing can be so important to your financial health, and how this is one of the best times to get started and invest.

I think you will be surprised at some of the reasons. Some that you may not have thought about.

Section 3 is called "Basic Information About The Stock Market." And we really mean basic information here -- just what you need to know to get started and no more. And we describe this in terms you already understand.

Here's an example for you right now. Have you ever wondered what the New York Stock Exchange is? You hear it mentioned in the news all the time. And you probably know it has something to do with stocks. But what is it?

Well, you know what an auction is, right? And that is all the New York Stock Exchange is. It's just an auction. It's where you will buy many of your stocks. See there. You already have a clue about stock exchanges. Because we introduced the idea with something you already understand. An auction.

And we did it in one sentence - "It's just an auction." Because we wrote the right sentence. We thought about what you already know before we started explaining. Then we built on that. It takes skill and effort to write in this manner. That's why you haven't run into it before.

Section 4 is called "What You Need To Get Started." You really only need one thing to get started. And that's a stock market account. Just like you need a checking account to hold your money and do your banking, you need a stock market account to hold your stocks and do your investing. See there, we did it again, didn't we. We started with something you know - a checking account. And then we related it to a stock market account.

We'll tell you how you can open a stock market account. And once you've done this, you're one click away from getting started. You can open your stock market account with a single phone call to a broker. And they will be happy to help you set it up. And I'll even tell you which online broker I have used successfully for years.

Here's the other good news. You only need to do this once. Then you're good to go.

Section 5 is called "How To Pick Good Stocks." Okay, now that you have an account, you will want to invest in your stocks. But which stocks should you buy? Here's the good news. You don't really need to do all kinds of complicated analysis if you don't want to. Because there are many great sources for stock recommendations.

We'll show you a number of these sources. Some are free. And some are newsletters that cost a modest amount of money. I think you will be surprised at how modest the subscription prices are for some of them.

I subscribe to them today. And I even subscribed to them when I was a financial consultant and stockbroker licensed with the New York Stock Exchange. As a stockbroker, you can imagine how many resources I had available to me. But I still used the resources I show you in this book. I'll give you the names of a couple of them, and where you can sign up if you want to go that route.

Then in Section 6 we get into "How To Buy And Sell Stocks." The steps to buy and sell are similar. We'll start by walking you through how to buy your first stock. And with your new online account you can do this in seconds, with the click of a mouse.

And like magic, someone, somewhere in the world, will sell you that stock. Similarly, you can sell it in seconds if you decide to. How good is that? Compare it to how long it takes, and difficult it is, to sell a house (weeks, months, years), for example. You can typically sell a stock in seconds. And we'll walk you through that too.

Section 7 is called "Protecting Your Stock Investments." This is mainly about when to sell. And it is the hardest question in investing. Not knowing when to sell causes people to take big losses in the stock market. Perhaps you have experienced this as well. But do you know that there is a simple technique that will keep you from having big losses? If you do this, you will be way ahead of most investors.

It's a simple, effective and important technique. We use it because, historically, over time, the stock market tends to go up, and your wealth increases. But it doesn't go up in a straight line. Sometimes the market and stocks go down for a while. Like the investors and employees at ENRON experienced. Had they used this one technique, and another one we show you as well, they would not have suffered catastrophic losses where most of them got completely wiped out!

But you can protect against this. And we'll show you how.

So Who Am I And Why Should You Listen To Me?

So who am I and how can I help you with stock investing? Well, the short answer is I'm a former financial consultant and stockbroker licensed with the New York Stock Exchange. And I actually made money following the crash of 2008.

You remember the crash of 2008, right? The housing bubble went bust, the stock market came unglued, and millions of investors watched in horror as their stocks plummeted — and their hopes and dreams went up in smoke. Looking at a key market index of that period, stocks fell a whopping 38%. But many investors did far worse, losing half or more of their money.

Virtually everyone was affected, and I'm not here to tell you I ran the 2008 gauntlet unscathed.

But by 2008 I was far different than the average stock investor. The crash of 2008 presented incredible opportunities for those who knew how to seize them. So it was during those dark days that I made some of my best investments ever, and ultimately increased the value of my portfolio by 2 1/2 times.

But that was a far cry from how I started.

I started out knowing nothing. As a young man, I often wondered how people made money investing, and how the stock market worked. Decades ago, before calculators were even invented, I recall sitting down one night in my one bedroom apartment. And with pencil and paper, I manually calculated interest on my meager savings account, to see how long it would take to build wealth. And the answer was that I simply couldn't do it that way.

I was disappointed, and puzzled. How did some people grow so much wealth?

Slowly, the answer came to me. And it was that stock investing was a big part of the answer. So I began investing in a stock. But my first investment wasn't so great. It did well at first, but then I watched helplessly as my stock portfolio, consisting of just one stock, dwindled in front of my eyes. And although the solutions are obvious to me today, I wouldn't have known much what to do back then, even if I'd tried.

Does this story have a familiar sound to you? I was, perhaps, an investor just like you.

Years later I became a financial consultant and licensed stock broker working for a large broker dealer in the US. And through much research, study, trial and error, I began to understand the answer to my basic question.

And if I could do that, starting from such a humble beginning, and making so many mistakes, you can too.

So let's look at how the stock market can increase your wealth. Let's get to the basic question. And that is, "Why invest in stocks?"

2

WHY INVEST IN STOCKS

So why bother investing in stocks? What's in it for you?

And the answer is that stock investing can increase your wealth and income over time when done properly.

It does this for you in a number of ways.

For example, much has been made of the fact that there is a widening wealth and income gap in the US. You hear this in the news all the time. What they are talking about is the widening gap between the people in the top 10 percent of income earnings, and the bottom 90 percent. And all the facts bear this out. There is, indeed, a widening gap.

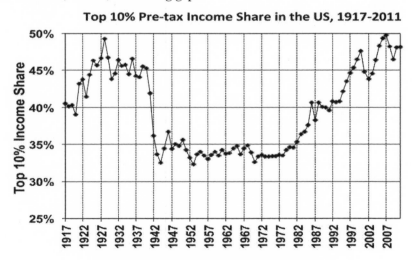

Figure 2-1. Top 10% Pre-tax Income Share
Source: Piketty and Saez, UC Berkeley

The income gap is the highest it's been since the early 1920's. And the same can be said for the wealth gap, which has not been so high since 1927. So wouldn't it be a good idea to do what the top 10 percent are doing -- to tap into that wealth and income too?

So what are the wealthy doing to make this happen? Well, most of them are business owners.

Warren Buffett and Bill Gates are two of the wealthiest people in the world. And it's not a coincidence that they are wealthy AND business owners. As of 2015, Bill Gates, who started Microsoft, had a net worth estimated at $77,534,032,783. Yes, you read that right. His net worth is over $77 billion dollars.

And here's another interesting fact for you. Warren Buffett, who started a company called Berkshire Hathaway, is also one of the greatest stock investors and businessmen of all time. One of the stocks his company owns is Coca Cola. He owns a lot of it, and he's owned it for a long time.

Coca Cola, like many other successful companies, pays part of their profits each year to their stockholders. Can you guess how big that check is that they pay to Warren Buffett every year? Well, as of 2013, his annual check was $448,000,000. That's right, $448 million dollars. Just for that year. And his checks will probably grow and be even greater in future years.

By the way, these checks are called dividend checks. That's some dividend check, yes? We'll discuss stocks that send dividend checks to you later in the book.

But the lesson here is that the wealthy own companies that increase their wealth. They are business owners. And owning stocks, like Coca Cola for example, is one of the easiest ways to become a business owner.

So let's explore this idea further. Because maybe we should be doing this too.

They Are The Easiest Way To Become A Business Owner

So let's say that again. Owning stocks is the easiest way to become a business owner.

When you buy a stock, you become a business owner. Really. So what does that mean? Well, as a business owner, instead of working for someone else, to increase their wealth, other people are working for you... to increase your wealth.

And these people, employees, go to work every day, voluntarily, to increase your wealth. Just like you probably go to work every day.

And they take care of making and selling the products and services, doing all the accounting, keeping the stores or offices running, advertising, and all the other things that are necessary to run a profitable business. Or put another way, they do all the things you would have to do if you started your own company.

And over time, they get more customers, and increase sales and profits, and make the company more valuable year after year.

What's so great about all of this is you don't have to do any of the work. They take care of it.

All you have to do is buy an ownership stake in the company. And as the company becomes more valuable, and generates more business, your stake, or stock (same thing) in the company becomes more valuable. Even better, many of these companies will send you a check, usually every three months, for your part of the profits. As we mentioned earlier, this is known as a dividend check. It's called dividend because they divided up the profits and sent you your part.

Why would they do this nice thing for you? Because you are one of the business owners. You own part of the company. So you own part of the profit. And the company, and all of its wonderful employees, are working hard every day to increase how much profit and money you make.

Contrast this to your experience as an employee. Your employer is doing their best to keep expenses low and pay you just enough to keep you, and no more. They are not actively working to increase your pay. That's an expense. They are doing everything possible to keep expenses low, so that they can make money for the business owners. And who are the business owners? You know the answer to that by now. They are the stock owners.

So which side of the table do you want to sit on? The employee side, where they are working to keep expenses low (that's you and your salary)?

Or the stock owner side, where they are working as hard as possible to create more profits and wealth for you?

I'm thinking the owner side of the table is best, aren't you? And the simple way to be on that good side of the table is to own stocks.

Now understand, not every business goes through the happy growth scenario I described. Some are not well run, and some fail. But there are many good companies that are well run, and succeed. And you can become an owner by buying their stock.

There's one final point to understand. And that is that even with good companies, not every year is as profitable as other years. Some year's profits are up, and some years they are down. But over time, these stocks, and the stock market, just keep making more money and becoming more valuable. Which means your part of the company, and profits, keeps getting more valuable too.

So let's take a look at this. How much has the stock market grown over time?

The Stock Market Has A Great Return Over 100 Years

Owning stocks in the stock market has returned more to investors than most other investments. On average, the stock market has grown 8% year by year.

But what does that mean to you?

Well, it means that if you invested $10,000, then nine years later it would be worth $20,000. Your investment would have doubled in nine years. So that is $10,000 in free money that you didn't have to work for. The money just grew on its own while you were living your life, day by day.

Now that 8% number I just used is a general guideline. And it's a pretty good guideline. However, it varies depending on what types of stocks and time frame you choose. For example, by one measure, over the last 87 years, stocks in large companies have averaged a whopping 11.8 percent a year.

Other common measures indicate the overall stock market has increased from 7 - 10% a year. And yet another measure states it has returned on average 8% per year.

By taking all of these historical measures into consideration, I tend to use 8% a year as a general guide. So let's go with that. And here is a chart that shows the overall trend of the market since before 1920.

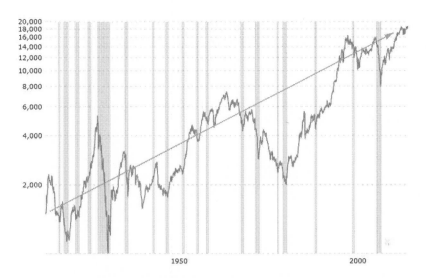

Figure 2-2. Dow Jones 100 Year Historical Chart
Source: Macrotrends.net

Now compare that to the average savings account, which pays you a measly 0.06 percent. Or worse yet, some of the nation's biggest banks pay rates even lower, as low as 0.01%.

Put another way, investment in stocks, using our 8% guideline, could DOUBLE YOUR MONEY in 9 years. But using the .01 interest on savings from the big banks it would take 7,200 years to double your money.

That's a huge difference in speed to create wealth. So now do you understand why the wealthy own businesses and stocks? That's a pretty compelling reason to be invested in the stock market, wouldn't you say? Clearly the wealthy understand this difference. And now you do too.

Okay - so I used two extreme investments for comparison. There are also government Treasury bonds you could invest in, which have averaged 3.6 percent. But it would still take 20 years to double your money. And try getting that return today, when they are actually much lower.

And while we're at it, let's do one more comparison in the stock market. Let's look at the return over the past 87 years for small companies. It's a whopping 16.5 percent. Or put another way, you would double your money in 4.4 years.

Now remember, these are just averages. As the chart shows, stocks may go up more in some years, and they will lose money in others. But over time, with good stocks, it's clear how the wealthy grow their wealth more quickly than the average person.

It's because they are invested in stocks and businesses that grow their wealth mush faster than those who are not invested. They are being smarter with their money.

And there's another way they are smarter with their money too. Remember when we mentioned earlier that some stocks pay you dividends? That is to say, they send you a check every three months for your portion of the company profits. Well, you won't be surprised to find out that the wealthy are on to that game as well.

So let's get into that now. Let's talk about dividend paying stocks.

NOTE: Most companies that pay dividends will send you a check every three months; that is to say every quarter. So I say three months throughout the book to keep things simple. But a few companies only pay dividends once a year. And some companies pay out dividend checks every month.

I really like that monthly idea, don't you? Now that's starting to feel like a real paycheck. And isn't that a nice concept - getting a monthly paycheck you don't have to work for. If that idea intrigues you, you can learn all about it in my book <u>Your Future Paychecks And Raises – Get Dividend Checks In Your Mailbox Paid To The Order Of You</u>.

Think Of Stocks As Money Machines

Here's how I like to think about dividend stocks. I like to think of them as money machines.

Wouldn't it be nice if you could just go down to Walmart and buy a money machine for $49.95? And the little money machines were advertised to create $.50 every three months. That would be like 4 cents a week. And they would just dump this money out on the floor.

And you could buy as many money machines as you wanted. Maybe every week you would buy another one. So in a year you would have fifty-two little money machines working for you, and all of them just dumping out more money.

And you just set your little money machines in a closet and forget about them. And every week they would each dump out four cents on the closet floor.

So after the first week you'd have 4 cents laying on the floor from the first money machine. The next week you buy another, so now you have two money machines. So you would get 8 cents more that week, on top of the 4 cents from the first week. The next week, three machines, so you'd get 12 more cents, on and on for fifty-two weeks. So at the end of the first year, you'd have over 5,700 pennies just laying all over the floor.

What a mess. But that's a $57 mess.

Now you can spend that $57 on anything you want to. It's your money. It's all from your money machines that you bought and paid for.

Or here's a thought. You take most of that $57 and buy one more money machine. Why not, it's paid for. The other money machines bought it for you (and you have $7 left over). So really, you can think of it as a free money machine. Now you have money machines buying money machines for you. What a great idea.

So now you have 53 money machines sitting in the closet. But it gets better. Because maybe next year all of your money machines start dumping out a little more money than they did last year — let's say $.55 every three months instead of $.50 like last year.

At the end of the second year you'd have 11660 pennies laying all over the floor (55 X 53 X 4). That's over $116. Now you can buy two more money machines. And the machines keep on increasing how many pennies each one dumps out by a little bit more each year.

That's a pretty good deal. Your money machines are giving you more and more money. They are even helping you buy more money machines for free. And you aren't having to do any work.

And we haven't even talked about the fact that after a couple of years, the price of the money machines goes up because more people want to buy them. Because other people like free money too. So now the ones you own are worth more than you paid for them. Maybe they are all worth $55 instead of the $49.95 you paid for them.

So now you have fifty-five money machines that you paid $49.95 for (let's just say $50 to keep the math easy). And they are now worth $55 each. So you have also made a profit of $5 per machine, times your fifty-five machines, for a profit of $275. Plus, you've gotten $121 from the fifty-five money machines this year, and $57 from the year before, for a total profit of $453. And the money machines will keep dumping out more money every year, and probably keep going up in value.

You paid $2600 for these money machines (you bought the first 52 at $50). And they have already paid you back $453 in value. You can see that at some point in time in the future they will have completely paid you back the $2600. And after that, everything is free money, year after year.

That's how dividend stocks work. They give you income - that's all the pennies laying on your floor. And over time their value goes up, so they give you growth too.

Interestingly, a share of Walmart stock would cost about as much as one of our fictitious money machines we said we bought at Walmart. And one share of Walmart stock would pay you about $.50 in dividends every three months, just like in our money machine example. So you can think of buying a share of Walmart stock as buying a money machine.

And just like the value of our money machines grew over time, the value of Walmart stock grows too. So you can think of Walmart as a stock that grows. And you can think of it as a stock that pays you income. Because Walmart pays a dividend.

So let's think about this for a minute. You can go out and spend your dividend money on a dinner at a restaurant, which is gone as soon as you eat it.

Or you can buy more shares of Walmart stock with it, i.e. buy more money machines.

Nothing against nice dinners, I enjoy them myself. I'm just saying they lose value instantly.

But your money machines become worth more over time. And they dump out more money every three months, year after year.

Are you beginning to get the picture? This is what the wealthy do. They spend their money on stocks, on money machines. And that's a good reason to invest in stocks, don't you think?

And here's another reason. It has to do with milk, roadrunners and gasoline. I'll bet you didn't see that one coming.

Note that in reality, some years the stock price (the value of your money machines) may not go up, and maybe even go down, and in some years it will go up even more than our example. But most of the time it will keep paying you dividends. And over time, on average, the shares of good stocks will keep moving up.

Stocks Beat The Robbing Effects Of Inflation

So now we know that stocks, like money machines, help increase your wealth. And here's another thing they help you with as well. They help you keep ahead of the robbing effects of inflation.

Inflation is a serious threat to you ever accumulating wealth. On average, it will reduce your purchasing power by about 3% a year. This is not some theoretical concept. It is very real. You can easily see it in the price of basic things you buy, considered necessities by most -- like milk, gasoline and automobiles.

For example, I recall back in the 70's when you could buy a quart of milk for a dime. Today that quart of milk cost $1.99.

Or take the cost of automobiles. I paid $4000 for a Plymouth Roadrunner back in the late 60's. It was one of those muscle cars with a big engine. Ok, hey, I was a young man back then, and a muscle car seemed like a necessity. But the point is that today, a similar car will cost you $30,000 or more.

And one other example is the cost of gasoline. Back in the early 70's, a gallon of gas in Springfield, Missouri cost a quarter. That's right, twenty-five cents a gallon. Today, that same gallon cost you $3.00.

Those are HUGE increases in prices over those decades. What's even worse is the average worker's salary has not gone up as fast during this time and in many cases it's stayed the same. So these basic necessities, things that you have to buy to live day to day, take more of your paycheck every year.

You are losing purchasing power. That's why so many people feel like they are losing ground. Because they are. And this point becomes even more important when you have to live off of your investments in retirement, and prices keep going up.

But there is one thing you can buy, that on average, has gone up in value during that time. And that is stocks. This is one of the reasons we see the widening gap in wealth between the top 10% and the bottom 90%. The top 10% have much more of their wealth in stocks. The bottom 90% have much less in stocks.

We mentioned earlier that on average, the price of stocks has gone up by 8% a year over the last 90 years. So even with 3% inflation, the wealthy top 10 percent of the population are increasing their wealth and purchasing power by 5% a year.

How did I get that 5% number? Because the wealthy make 8% with their stocks and they lose 3% to inflation. So they are still increasing their purchasing power by 5% a year, while others without stocks are losing 3% a year.

So when you own stocks, not only are you keeping up with the robbing effects of inflation, but you are beating it and increasing your wealth.

Now do you see why there is a widening wealth and income gap? And doesn't this seem like another good reason to invest in stocks?

So here's the good news, and our last reason to invest in stocks. It has to do with my disappointing walk across a street in downtown St. Louis years ago. And how things have changed in your favor since then.

Stock Investing Is Easier And Cheaper Than Ever Before

The good news is that it's easier to invest in the stock market today than any time in history.

I remember decades ago when I wanted to invest in stocks. I worked in downtown St. Louis, and there were a number of stockbroker businesses in the downtown area. And a new one had just opened right across the street from where I worked. How convenient, I thought.

I had almost no money back then, but thought to at least buy one share of stock I had read about for $80. That was all I had. But I thought, if I just got started, I could buy more stock over time.

That's a great thought and technique by the way - to just get started, no matter how small the amount.

So one day on my lunch hour, I crossed the street with high hopes to buy my stock and start my investing plan. I walked into the new stockbroker office, and a broker came over and asked if he could help me. This turned out to be a rhetorical question, because as soon as I said I wanted to buy one share of stock for $80, he lost all interest. Not only that, he got a look of real disdain on his face and told me, not so gently, that they didn't deal with small amounts like that.

I left his office feeling a little bit embarrassed. I was clearly small change in his eyes. I had crossed the street with high hopes. But I was re-crossing the street feeling kind of defeated.

But it's probably just as well, because back then, individual brokers charged commissions of $65 and up for a purchase. Their only other competition was with other full service brokers like them. This was way before online discount brokers came on the scene. So since you literally had to go through one of them to buy shares of stock, they were all able to keep their commission rates high.

For the stock brokers, these were the glory days, as they controlled access to the markets.

For a small time investor like me, there was no glory in it at all. They wouldn't even deal with me. So, like I said, I walked out of his office pretty disappointed. And with a pretty bad taste in my mouth about the stock market, investing in stocks, the broker, and his business.

And I pretty much gave up on the idea for a while after that awkward experience.

But over the years, the whole scene changed. And it changed in favor of stock investors like you and me. Because, with the advent of the internet, came the creation of online stock brokers. And discount online brokers as well.

This meant I could open an online account on the internet with a small amount like $100 to get started. And I didn't have to deal with a snooty stockbroker. And I could do my own buying and selling too, online, at a much cheaper commission - like $10, versus $65 or more in the old days.

So the good news is that there are a number of these online discount brokers today. And I use one of them all of the time, to buy and sell my shares of stock. We'll get into that later in the book.

And to be fair, there are many good stockbrokers you can use today as well, if you want to pay for their services. The guy I used in my example was just not one of them. Just my luck, I started with him first.

But for now, just remember, stock investing is cheaper and easier to do than at any time in history. So you don't need to deal with all those expenses today. And it's all because of the online discount brokers.

So now that we know that stock investing is a good thing to do, and cheaper and easier than ever, let's learn something about stocks. For example, just what is a stock anyway?

3

BASIC INFORMATION ABOUT THE STOCK MARKET

No doubt whenever you've heard about stocks and the stock market, you've felt blitzed with all kinds of technical terms. It's like people are speaking Greek, and it can be discouraging. After all, you just want to make a simple stock investment to make money, not learn a second language, right?

So here's the good news. You don't really need to know all of this technical

Interestingly enough, some investment terms really are Greek, like "beta" for example. No wonder people find investing confusing. For the curious, in stock terms, beta just means how much and how fast your stock goes up or down. Some stocks move slowly, others move fast and erratic. But we don't really need to get into that here.

stuff to get started. Actually, you only need to understand a few basic things. And when I say basic, I mean basic.

All you need to know is what a share of stock is, how to pick good ones, and where and how you can buy and sell them.

Simple, right? That's all you really want to know. So we'll leave all the technical gobbletygook for others, and just talk about what you need to know.

So let's start with the most basic thing first. And that is, just what is a share of stock?

What Is A Share Of Stock
When you invest in stocks, you are actually buying something called shares of stock. So what is a share of stock?

Well, let's think about a pizza pie. And let's say you and your friends all chip in and buy a pie together. So you will all share slices of the pizza pie. I just said the word "share," didn't I?

So you cut the pie into slices. And you share the slices with your friends. They each get their share of slices and you get your share.

Now let's say you and your friends want to buy a business together. Maybe a nice wine shop to go with the pizza. So you will all share in the business.

You cut (divide) the ownership of the business into slices (shares). And you share the ownership (slices, shares) with your friends. They each get their share and you get your share.

That's all a share of stock is. It's your slice (share) of the business. It's your share of the ownership. It's your share of the profits. It's your share.

Corporations slice their ownership up into shares also. And anyone can buy a share. Or you can buy more than one share. Just like our pizza example. Let's say the pizza cost $10 and you cut it into 10 slices. That's $1.00 a slice. That's the price of a share. If you were really hungry, you could have chipped in $2.00 so you would get two slices. So you would have bought two shares.

Of course, corporations are a lot bigger than a $10 pizza pie or your small business you started with your friends. So they cut the ownership of the corporation into millions of shares. And you can buy more than one share. You can buy 12 shares, or 100 shares, or a 1000 shares. You can buy as many shares as you want and can afford.

But it is exactly the same idea as the 10 shares of pizza pie above. You are buying your slice(s) of the corporate pie. You are buying your share(s).

So here's a real world example for you. Pizza Hut is one of the largest pizza companies in the world. They are owned by the YUM Brands Corporation.

Do you know how many shares they have divided their corporation into? (I don't really expect you to know this). They have 466,000,000 shares. Each share costs about $50. If you bought all of the shares it would cost over 23 billion dollars ($23,000,000,000) to buy the whole corporation.

That's a lot of money. So isn't it nice they slice the company up into many little shares so we can all afford to buy part of it?

So if you had $50 you could buy a share of YUM Brands Corporation. And you would just need to know one key thing to buy that share of stock?

You would need to know this: YUM.

Because YUM is the stock symbol for the YUM Brands Corporation. And you need to know the stock symbol in order to buy your share. So let's talk about stock symbols.

What Is A Stock Symbol

There are over 8000 different stocks that you can buy in the US. That's a lot of different stocks to deal with, and you can imagine there needs to be a simple way to identify each one of them.

So you often see stocks referred to as a short series of letters – like YUM, for example. Or MSFT, S or GOOG. This is called a stock symbol, and it's really pretty simple.

Note that these are sometimes also called ticker symbols, a throwback to the past when the stock prices printed on paper tapes, and made a ticking sound as they printed.

Each stock has a short, unique abbreviation assigned to it. No other stock has that abbreviation. Like we mentioned earlier, the abbreviation for YUM Brands Corporation is YUM. No other stock can use the abbreviation YUM. The abbreviation for Microsoft is MSFT. No other stock can use the abbreviation MSFT.

So when you see YUM, that ALWAYS means the YUM Brands Corporation. When you see MSFT, that ALWAYS means people are talking about shares of Microsoft stock. Or when you see S, that is ALWAYS Sprint. And when you see GOOG, that is Google.

A stock symbol is just a short abbreviation of the stock, so people don't have to key in the entire name. Imagine if you worked in the financial industry and had to write out the full company name every time you were buying or selling stocks during the day. That's just too much work. So you would start abbreviating.

And that's all a stock symbol is really – just a unique abbreviation for a stock. It's that simple.

Here are some other companies you are probably familiar with, and their stock symbols.

AAPL - Apple Computers
HSY - Hershey's chocolate bars
CLX - Clorox bleach
F - Ford Motor Company
T - AT&T telephone company
MOO - I love this one. This is a fund of agriculture stocks. These people
are not without a sense of humor - chuckle.

From now on in this book, whenever we refer to a stock, we will also show its
stock symbol in parentheses like this... Apple Computers (AAPL).

And it's easy to find the symbol for a stock if you don't know it. Just search
for it in a search engine like Google. For example, to find the stock symbol
for Apple Computers, just key in "Stock symbol for apple stock" or "Ticker
symbol for apple stock."

Or   you   can   go   here   https://en.wikipedia.org/wiki/List_of_S%
26P_500_companies to see a list of the top 500 companies in the US and their
stock symbol (or ticker symbol – same thing). By the way, this list of the top
500 companies is known as the S&P 500. You may have heard people mention the S&P 500 on news shows. S&P stands for Standard & Poor's, an organization that has been providing financial market information for more than
150 years.

Simple, isn't it?

So now that we know how to identify a stock by its stock symbol, let's talk
about the different kinds of stocks.

What Kinds Of Stocks Can You Buy

There are many different kinds of stocks you can invest in. But they all tend
to fall into one of two groups.

You can buy stocks that you think will grow in value over time. These are
called **growth stocks**. Or you can buy stocks that pay you income. These are
called **income stocks**.

You will also hear the term "growth and income stocks." These stocks do
both - they grow AND pay you income, although they typically grow a bit
slower than pure growth stocks.

Most people think about growth stocks when you mention investing. They've
heard a story about a friend that bought stock in a new company. And the

company really took off, became very large and profitable, and now their shares are worth a lot of money.

It's an exciting kind of "get rich quick" story. And so everyone is out chasing the next big growth stock, trying to make this happen for themselves.

And this type of growth can really happen -- over time. For example, had you bought $1000 worth of Microsoft stock in 1993, your shares would have grown to be worth about $20,000 by 2015.

That's not too shabby. The company, and its shares of stock, really grew in value over time. So you can see why people invest in growth stocks. And like I said, this is the typical way that people think about stock investing. They only think of how much the stock will grow in value. Perhaps this is the way you view stocks too.

But there's another way to think of stock investing; another type of stocks to consider besides growth stocks. And they are income stocks. These stocks pay you money.

You see, most companies start out as growth stocks. And in the beginning, they don't pay any of their profits to the stockholders. They use those profits to grow their business rapidly in the early years of their life. And if you are a stockholder, you get to go along for that profitable ride.

But eventually, after all the years of rapid growth, their growth slows down. That's because they have reached most of the market with their products. They are still profitable, earning income every year. But there are less ways for them to grow their business. They are now mature, well established companies. And they need less of their income to grow the business. So they start paying their stockholders part of their profits.

As we mentioned earlier, these payments to you, the stockholder, are called dividends. You can think of dividends as the company "dividing" up the profits of the company, and sending them to the business owners.

Once a company matures to this point, people start thinking of it more as an income stock, instead of a growth stock. So when they buy shares in it, invest in it, they are thinking more about how much it will pay them in dividend checks, instead of how much it will grow in value.

These income stocks have been less popular in recent years, probably due to all the phenomenal growth stories people have heard about stocks like Microsoft, or Apple. That's understandable. Growth stocks are exciting. They have a great story, and you hear about them all the time in the news.

But it wasn't always this way. In years past, the first thing investors would ask when their broker recommended a stock was how much it would pay them -- what were the dividends. It wasn't a crazy question. And they were in good company by asking it. Indeed, John Rockefeller, founder of Standard Oil, said that the greatest pleasure he got was when he received his dividend checks from his stocks. So Rockefeller certainly thought income stocks were important.

And with income stocks, the company really will send you a check in the mail for your share of the profits, typically every three months. If you own their stock, you will receive a dividend check. Which you can deposit in your bank account. And spend how you like. The money is yours. Because you are one of their business owners.

Practically speaking, most stockowners just set it up where the money is directly deposited into their stock account. It's just easier than getting a check every three months and having to deposit it into their checking account. And they can even set it up where the dividend will automatically buy more of the stock, thus increasing their investment and future dividends. This is called dividend reinvestment.

And over time, the dividend checks can be quite significant. As we mentioned earlier, Warren Buffett gets a Coca Cola dividend check for $448,000,000 every year. Clearly, Coke is it!

So income stocks are certainly something to consider.

Now, dividend stocks tend to be less glamorous and more boring. You won't hear all the exciting stories about them in the news. But like the great mutual fund manager Peter Lynch said, his perfect stock "sounds dull… and it does something dull."

Think of Clorox in this context. You know, the company that makes bleach for your laundry. That's pretty dull and boring. But they pay a dividend every year. And people are going to buy bleach and wash their clothes, year after year. So you will keep getting dividends from them, year after year.

Here are some more of Peter's favorite boring stocks from the past. Try payroll manager Automatic Data Processing (ADP). Or Consolidated Rock - a concrete maker (now CalMat Co., CLWY). Very dull. Very boring. Although the last one, Consolidated Rock, strikes me as somewhat humorous, like something out of a Flintstones cartoon.

But people will always keep washing their clothes. And payrolls will always need to be paid. And the world is not going to quit using concrete. So these are steady, reliable businesses to invest in.

Here's one more example. It's Microsoft (MSFT). It started out as a super growth stock. Their Windows operating system was innovative and exciting at the time they introduced it. But today, most people already use Windows. And Microsoft is considered kind of boring.

And guess what. Now that their big growth phase is behind them, Microsoft pays a dividend. So Microsoft is a great example of a growth stock that matured and turned into an income stock. But just because it's boring now, don't ignore it. Because Microsoft is a cash-gushing money machine. They will probably be around for a long time, and keep paying bigger and bigger dividends. For many stockholders, Microsoft has been a great investment.

Interestingly, Microsoft's competitor Apple (AAPL) has also matured and pays a dividend. But Apple is not considered a boring stock. Their flashy marketing has kept them at the forefront of the public's attention. Indeed, customers get in lines for hours in advance to buy their latest product. And Apple, now an income stock, has also been a great investment.

So basically, there are two kinds of stocks you can invest in. They are growth stocks and income stocks. And over time many growth stocks turn into income stocks.

Most people invest in both types, as do I. But I tend to favor income stocks. Because they pay me money to do so. And they usually keep growing to some degree as well. So I feel like I am getting the best of both worlds.

So now that we know about these two types of stocks, growth and income, we just need to know one more basic thing. And that is, where do we go to buy them?

Where Do You Buy Stocks
So where do you buy stocks?

And the answer is that you buy them at places called exchanges. Like the New York Stock Exchange.

Now that may sound a bit intimidating, but really, the New York Stock Exchange is just an auction. You know, like an auction where there's a guy talking real fast to a bunch of buyers to sell Grandma Mable's rocking chair, and all her other possessions, so she can move to Florida to be near her grandkids.

And in her auction, different people keep bidding a higher and higher price until someone discovers they bid the highest price and now they own the rocking chair.

Similarly, that's all the New York Stock Exchange (NYSE) is, really. An auction.

But instead of selling rocking chairs, they sell shares of stock in different companies. And whoever bids the highest price just bought the stock.

Also understand that the NYSE is an auction on steroids. Because instead of one auctioneer selling one thing at a time to a bunch of people, it's a bunch of people selling and buying stocks to and from each other all at once.

Until recently, the brokers at the New York Stock Exchange were all standing out in the open on the floor, shouting and crying out buy and sell orders to each other, all at the same time, and making all kinds of noise.

This is why it was called the "open outcry" system. Really. And it was so noisy many of them used hand signals to communicate with one another.

It was one gigantic, noisy bunch of auctions all happening at once on the floor of the exchange as they traded stocks with each other. So you won't be surprised when I tell you they were called "floor traders."

I say they WERE called floor traders, because today this isn't done so much. Instead, the traders are buying and selling and holding all their simultaneous auctions with each other on their computers.

But it's still the same thing — just not as noisy. It's an auction. Kind of like E -Bay. But much more and much faster.

So when you ask to buy or sell a stock, one of these traders gets your order and jumps into the auction to buy or sell it for you. And you get the best price that another person is willing to pay or sell for.

And just like an auction, your shares of stock don't have a fixed price. They are only worth what someone will pay at the big auction. But we will get more into that later.

For now, all you need to remember is that the New York Stock Exchange is just a big auction. And they sell shares of stock at their auction.

So that's where you buy stocks. At an exchange. And you probably won't be surprised to learn that there are other exchanges as well.

For example, you may have heard about the NASDAQ and OTC and wondered what they are. Well, they are just other, different exchanges where you can buy and sell stocks. They are just other auctions.

But they tend to sell different kinds of stocks than those that the New York Stock Exchange (abbreviated as the NYSE) sells.

Kind of like Macy's Department Stores sells higher end merchandise than Walmart. And kind of like different kinds of auctions sell different kinds of things.

For example, some auctions sell expensive things like fine art. Like Sotheby's, the famous fine art auction where you often hear in the news how they sold a painting for millions of dollars.

Other auctions sell cheaper things, like Grandma Mable's rocking chair at her estate sale (not saying anything against Grandma Mable here). Just think of some fast talking auctioneer out at her house, with all her things out in the yard.

And maybe some auctions sell more technical things, like computers, let's say.

So we already talked about the **New York Stock Exchange (NYSE).** It's a big auction that sells shares of stock in the big, expensive companies. It's kind of like the expensive, fine art auction. Some stocks that are sold on the NYSE are Ford Motor Company, AT&T, etc.

You would never find Grandma Mable's rocking chair at a fine art auction. So, similarly, there's another exchange (auction) that sells smaller, cheaper companies.

It's called the **Over The Counter Market (OTC).** It's more like the lower priced rocking chair / furniture auction. I'm not knocking the companies that are sold there. They are just much smaller companies, many of which are just getting started. Some of these startup companies can offer incredible profit opportunities if you have good research and pick the right one.

Most of these OTC stocks you've never heard of. For example, I have invested in one called TapImmune (TPIV). They are a startup drug company developing a vaccine to cure certain forms of cancer. They are just getting started, and many small startup stocks like this never make it. They can be high risk, and usually have very cheap prices per share. For example, I bought many shares of them at $.09 a share. But if they make it, they could make it big.

And then there's an auction that sells mainly shares of stock in technology companies — like Microsoft. It's kind of like our computer auction. It's called the **NASDAQ, which stands for National Association of Securities Dealers Automated Quotations.** Say that fast three times. Or do what everyone else does and just say Naz' Dack.

Some companies listed on the NASDAQ exchange are Apple (AAPL) and Microsoft (MSFT). These are clearly technology companies.

So your stocks are bought and sold in different exchanges (auctions). Which means you will buy and sell your stocks on different exchanges, depending on what type of stocks they are.

Now, if that's starting to sound a little complicated, here's the good news. You don't really need to worry about what exchange your stock is being sold on. Because when you go to buy a stock, your order will automatically go to the right exchange. For example, if you place an order to buy Microsoft (MSFT) shares, it will automatically go to the NASDAQ exchange.

If you place an order to buy Sprint stock, it will automatically go to the New York Stock Exchange (NYSE). And if you were to place an order to buy TapImmune (TPIV), it would automatically go to the OTC exchange.

Interestingly, as I was writing this book, TapImmune (TPIV) left the small stock OTC Exchange and moved up to the NASDAQ Exchange, where stocks have to cost $5 or more. But I still just enter TPIV if I want to buy more shares, like I did in the past. And now my order is automatically sent to the NASDAQ, instead of the OTC exchange.

Isn't that easy? Wouldn't it be nice if everything was that simple (like understanding your phone or medical insurance bill)?

Okay, so now you know that stocks are bought and sold at exchanges.

Now to the important question. And that is, how do you find good stocks to buy?

4

HOW TO FIND GOOD STOCKS TO BUY

Before you decide to buy a stock, you want to remember that you are buying a business. You are becoming a business owner. Granted, you are buying just a portion of a business. And probably a very small portion at that.

HOW MUCH OF THE BUSINESS DO YOU OWN? Let's say you are buying Microsoft (MSFT) stock. They have 7,990,000,000 shares (this is known as shares outstanding). That means the ownership of the company is sliced up into 7,990,000,000 parts. So if you decide to buy a share of Microsoft (MSFT) stock, you are buying just 1/7,990,000,000 of that company.

Even if you are buying 10 or 100 or 1000 shares, you are still buying a really small part of Microsoft. Compare that to Bill Gates, who owned 330 million shares in 2014 according to a Forbes article. That's about 4% of the company.

But none the less, you are still buying part of that business. And no smart business person would buy into a business without doing some research first.

They would want to know what the company's sales were, if their sales were increasing every year, how much profit those sales were creating, if profits were increasing every year, if the company was badly in debt, or had a lot of cash, and many other things.

Then they would decide if the company was worth buying.

Similarly, you need to know if a company's stock is worth buying.

But don't get discouraged about all this research, because there is an easy way to get it done. And that is to let someone else do it for you. And then see if they recommend buying the stock.

This is what I often do. And it will keep you from having to do hours of research on companies you want to invest in. Why not just get the advice and recommendations of people who do this for a living.

Now there are two ways to get these recommendations. One way is free, and the other you have to pay for. I do a bit of both, but prefer the paid way. I'll tell you some good sources for recommendations, both free and paid, in this chapter. Then you can choose what is best for you.

So let's start off with the free stock recommendations.

Free Stock Recommendations

There are a number of nightly television shows that give free stock recommendations.

One of these is Jim Cramer's show on CNBC called Mad Money. I like him and watch him frequently. But be warned — he is a pretty hyper-animated character. Personally, I think he should never drink coffee because the caffeine would make him even more hyper. On the other hand, his show is never boring, and quite entertaining.

Jim has been a very successful investor. And he gives specific stock recommendations. He's also very good at explaining things.

I've read his book *Getting Back To Even – Your Personal Economic Recovery Plan,* and it's quite good. I recommend it for those who want to get much deeper into the subject of stock investments.

And he has quite a following, so you don't actually have to watch his show every night to get his recommendations. There are a number of web sites that publish them. Here is one of them that you can check out at https://www.thestreet.com/mad-money/.

The other television show I watch often is Fast Money, also on CNBC. It's hosted by Melissa Lee, and who doesn't like watching Melissa? She moderates a panel of four other traders who discuss stocks, and at the end of the show, she asks each one of them for their final trade, i.e. a specific stock they would recommend.

These tips are also posted on their web site, so again, you don't need to watch this show every evening to keep up. You can see their site and recommendations at http://www.cnbc.com/id/17390482. Then look for a posting called Final Trade. Or in case the link changes, just Google "Fast Money Final

Trade" to see their latest recommendations.

There are, of course, many other free stock recommendation sources like these. But what I like about these two is they give you SPECIFIC recommendations, i.e. they say, "I would buy this specific stock." So that's a big advantage. Also, they provide great education—and entertainment. And there's nothing wrong with having fun while you learn, because you will do more of something that's fun and entertaining - and become a better investor.

The downside to these shows is that they may not follow-up on all of their stock picks in subsequent shows. So if their stock pick is going the wrong way, there may not be a follow-up to say you should sell it. However, we get into when to sell later on in the book, so this downside doesn't rule them out.

That said, I tend not to use these sources to pick most of my trades. I prefer to use financial newsletters that I subscribe to and pay for. That's because they can give a more thorough and deliberate stock analysis, since they're not restricted to a short segment of television time. And the paid newsletters definitely follow up with the status of their stock recommendations. Many will even send you email alerts when something unusual has happened to a recommended stock, or it is time to sell.

So let's take a look at these paid for stock recommendations. Let's look into financial newsletters.

Paid Stock Recommendations

Paying money for stock recommendations may be a new idea to you. It may even be something your brain kind of resists at first. But before you immediately rule it out, here are some things to consider.

First, you may be surprised at how inexpensive some newsletters are, and what a terrific value they can be for the money. Here's another good reason. With a newsletter, you don't feel like you're out there just guessing, and doing this all alone. It's like the newsletter writer is kind of in there with you. And they are, because they have a reputation to protect.

So when it comes to newsletter subscription prices, I typically buy newsletters that cost around $60 to $89 per year. But they are often on sale for $39 per year if you catch their specials and introductory offers. That's about nine lattes per year at Starbucks, and these newsletters can make you some "green" bucks.

NEWSLETTER PRICES - YIKES: When it comes to newsletter prices, they can range from free to up to $25,000 per year and more. We'll be avoiding the $25,000 per year variety. The latter are more for institutions or very wealthy investors.

I'll give you the names of two newsletters later that are under $50 each for an annual subscription. And you really only need one or two to help with your investing.

Remember, I was a financial consultant and licensed stockbroker at a large national broker dealer in the past. So I could do some of this research myself. And I had all kinds of free broker research available to me as well.

And I still bought these newsletters for myself. In my opinion, they are that good. So these days, I continue to take the easy road and buy specific newsletters. And I make many of my stock investments based on their recommendations.

Price consideration aside, I choose newsletters that have the following format. The format works for me, and it will be good for you as a beginning investor.

For example, the newsletter writer always tells a story about the recommendations they are making for that month. They describe the research they did, and why they think the stock is a good investment. They also discuss the risks that they considered.

And they ALWAYS end the article with a specific buy statement that looks like this. Example: ***Buy Sprint (NYSE: S) up to $5 a share and use a 25% trailing stop.***

Here's why this is good for you as a beginning investor. Even if you don't understand all of the analysis and research they describe in the story, you will know EXACTLY what to buy, and at what price, to take advantage of their recommendation.

In our example above, here's what they said about their Sprint recommendation.

- They told you to buy Sprint stock.

- They told you to not buy it for more than $5 a share.

- They told you what exchange the stock trades on "NYSE - the New York Stock Exchange."

- They told you the Stock symbol "S" (to use when placing your order).

- They even told you when to get out of the stock. "25% trailing stop - we'll get into that later."

What could be more specific? And easier? Really?

So if you are one of those people that skips to the end of a book to find out the ending, you could do the same here -- just skip the story and analysis, go straight to the recommendation, decide how many shares you want to buy and place the order.

I don't recommend that, because I think you will begin to learn more about stocks as you read the stories. Even if you don't get the whole thing, you will begin to understand more and more over time. And the stories are written in an interesting way.

I have friends who don't know much about stocks that I have shared some of these stock stories with, and they read them from top to bottom. They may not have understood the whole thing, but they get the general idea. And you will too.

And it gets better yet. Because when you buy one of these subscription newsletters, they will send you updates on how the stock is doing, and even special email alerts if the stock starts going bad.

So they do all the business research for you (saving you hours of hard work). And they tell you exactly what to buy and how much to pay. And they tell you when to get out.

Additionally, at the end of the newsletter, they have a list of all of their current recommendations, how they are doing, which ones you can still buy if you like, and the maximum price you should pay for them.

That pretty much covers everything you need to know, right?

I think you'll agree this is so much better than Uncle Harry's stock tip he tells you about at Thanksgiving after he's had a couple of drinks. Or the hot stock tip your buddy tells you about. Or the hot stock story that made the evening news. By the way, I've heard some of these newscasters (not the financial ones) can't even balance their expense accounts. And they are reporting hot stock tips? Interesting.

One final point. Some stock recommendations will not work out. It's impossible for these newsletters to have a 100% track record over time. So be aware of this. And know there are ways to minimize those losses, which we will cover later in the book.

But on balance, I think good newsletters really help improve your odds of stock investing success.

So with all that in mind, here are a couple of newsletters that fit my requirements. I have subscribed to both of them in the past and been happy with them. And one or both of them may be useful to you as well.

Two Of My Favorite Newsletters

There are literally hundreds of financial newsletters offered to the general public, and you could easily get lost in this publishing maze. So for now, I'm going to keep it simple and just mention two of them. They are *The Oxford Communiqué* and *The Oxford Income Letter*.

I first started seeing *The Oxford Communiqué* around 1995, so these newsletters have been around for a while and have a pretty good track record.

The newsletters are part of the Oxford Club, which began publishing under that name in the mid 1980's. If you are interested, here's a link to the history of the club and the newsletters - http://oxfordclub.com/the-oxford-clubs-beginnings/.

Both newsletters follow two of my key requirements. First, they give specific recommendations, i.e. they will say "Buy this stock up to this price." And second, they are quite reasonable in price, at around $49 for a year's subscription.

Compare that cost to using a full service broker. If you took one of his recommendations, and ask him to place the order for you, he would probably charge you $60 or more in commission - for that one order. There's nothing wrong with that if you don't want to place your orders in your own online account. I'm just showing you the newsletter price for an entire year as a comparison to that one-trade cost.

Full-Service Broker Commissions: These can vary considerably from one firm to another, ranging from $30 to $300 per trade, with the average around $120. Some full-service firms also have discount online brokers, and reduced broker-assisted commission rates ranging from $30 to $40 per trade.

So which newsletter should you look into? Well, you'll recall that earlier we said people can invest in stocks for their growth, or invest in stocks to get income. *The Oxford Communiqué* recommends mainly growth stocks, and as its name implies, *The Oxford Income Letter* recommends income stocks.

So if you are primarily interested in growth stocks, then *The Oxford Communiqué* is a good place to start. It's a full-service publication that does the research into solid growth stocks for you. Their Chief Investment Strategist is Alexander Green. He creates interesting and well researched descriptions of his recommendations, and uses a disciplined approach to limit risk, quite similar to what we recommend in the Protecting Your Stock Investments chapter of this book.

According to *The Oxford Communiqué,* they have helped subscribers score gains of 59% on iShares MSCI Hong Kong... 135% on Riverbed Technology... 48% on Managers Freemont Bond Fund... 65% on HMS Holdings... and many more.

And their track record with their recommendations in *The Oxford Communiqué* has earned them a "Top 10" rating by the prestigious *Hulbert Financial Digest.* So if you are into growth stocks, *The Oxford Communique* is a good newsletter to start out with.

You can get access to this newsletter and subscribe at http://oxfordclub.com/communique/.

Similarly, if you are more interested in stocks that will pay you income, *The Oxford Income Letter* is worth checking out. The interesting thing about income stocks is that most of them also grow, although typically slower, so in a sense you are getting the best of both worlds.

For example, looking at my latest *Oxford Income Letter,* they are recommending a technology stock that is currently paying a 7% dividend, and has continually increased its dividend over the past years. The stock price is very low, and there are good reasons to believe it will grow from here. So, like I said, best of both worlds.

Their Chief Income Strategist is Marc Lichtenfeld, and, as they say, he offers cutting edge insight every month on how to create an unbeatable income portfolio. He provides picks and analysis on dividend stocks, and provides updates on three groups of stock picks (stock portfolios), which you can follow depending on your objectives. These portfolios are...

The Retirement Catch-Up/High Yield Portfolio - with emphasis on current high yields.

The Instant Income Portfolio - with emphasis on income for today.

The Compound Income Portfolio Dividend - emphasizing reinvestment for tomorrow.

The portfolios look interesting, don't they? So if you are into income stocks, *The Oxford Income Letter* is a good newsletter to start out with. You can get access to this newsletter and subscribe if you like at http://oxfordclub.com/income-letter/.

To summarize, both *The Oxford Communique* and *The Oxford Income Letter* fit all of my criteria for good newsletters. There are many more newsletters out there, but these two are a good place to get started. And to emphasize that I eat my own cooking, I subscribe to both of these newsletters as of this writing. And I actually own some of the stocks recommended in their portfolios.

You can subscribe to both of them, or just one of them, depending on your investing needs and goals. Everyone's goals are different, so you will need to decide.

But if you just can't decide on which one to start with, I would probably start with *The Oxford Income Letter*. You will earn nice dividends on your investments, and many of them will probably grow in value as well.

So now that you know how to find good stocks to buy, you just need one more thing to get started. So let's talk about a stockbroker account.

5

WHAT YOU NEED TO GET STARTED

There's just one more thing you need to do before you can buy your first stock. And that is to open a stockbroker account.

Think of it this way. Just like you need a bank account to do your banking, you need a stockbroker account to do your stock investing.

You've probably had, and used, a bank account for years. So you're already familiar with banking accounts (checking, savings, etc.). **You keep your cash in your bank accounts.** And you make deposits, withdrawals, write checks and make transfers of that cash into and out of those accounts.

Similarly, **you keep your stocks in your stockbroker account** (and bonds, mutual funds, etc. - we'll focus on stocks to keep it simple). And you buy and sell stocks in that account. Interestingly, you also keep some cash for investments in that account, so that you can buy stocks. And when you sell a stock, the cash from that sale is put back into your broker account.

And once you have opened a stockbroker account, you can start investing in stocks. That is to say, you can start buying and selling stocks using that account.

To open a stockbroker account, you will need to choose a stockbroker. This is similar to when you opened your banking account. You had to choose a bank to open it with. So you may have looked at Bank of America, USBank, a regional or local bank, etc., and chosen one of them.

Similarly, you will need to choose a stockbroker to open an account with. I'll list a number of them for you, and even tell you which one I have used, quite satisfactorily, for years.

Choosing A Broker

When you choose a stockbroker (or broker) you will have to decide if you want a full-service broker or an online discount broker.

With a full-service broker, you pay the broker a commission to do your buying and selling for you. Typically, they may make stock recommendations as well. Your advantage with a full-service broker is that you won't have to learn how to place buy and sell orders, and you will have the assurance a professional is doing this for you. And you will have access to their advice and recommendations. Of course, brokers have to eat, so they will charge you commissions for this service.

Or you can open an online discount broker account and do all of your trading (buying and selling stocks) yourself. While that option is not free, as the name implies, the commissions for trading your online account run at a big discount to having a broker do the trades for you.

To give you an idea how big the discount is, a typical full service broker might charge you $60 or more to buy or sell a stock for you. Compare that to discount brokers. I have seen commissions advertised as low as $4.50. And I pay around $10 with my online discount broker. That's a big difference.

Some people start by using a full-service broker, then move on to trading their own online account. Or you can start right off with an online account. It depends on your level of confidence.

In my opinion, using a discount broker is fine for most individuals. Consider that millions of people trade online today, so it is not terribly difficult if you apply what you learn here. And most discount online brokers give you the option of talking to one of their live brokers to help you through a transaction if you get confused. They will probably charge you extra for that transaction, but you can watch and learn, and then do it yourself next time at the online discount fee.

So the rest of this book is oriented toward you doing your own trading in an online discount broker account. But even if you choose a full service broker to do this for you, all the information presented here is still valuable to you. That's because you will still want to understand what your full-service broker is telling you. And doing for you. And you will need to be able to tell them what you want them to do for you as well.

One final thought on brokers while you are choosing one. They should be friendly and helpful when you are opening your account with them. A good broker should also be accessible to you and return your calls. And a full-service broker should periodically keep you up to date on the status of your account, and they should take the time to explain any transactions that you don't understand. So if they aren't helpful when you are opening your account, choose another broker.

Of course, brokers are busy like the rest of us, so unless you have good reason, you shouldn't be calling them every five minutes — just call when you need to.

List Of Online Brokers

There are many good online discount brokers you can use. Here are some thoughts about them for you.

There are online discount brokers and super discount brokers. I tend to avoid the super discount guys. I had trouble with a super discount broker in my commodity options trading past, so I favor the more run of the mill, average discount brokers.

Some brokers that fit this description are ...

TDAmeritrade - www.tdameritrade.com
Scottrade - www.scottrade.com
E*Trade - www.etrade.com
Fidelity Investments - www.fidelity.com
Charles Schwab - www.schwab.com

Setting up and keeping an account with these brokers should be free, and the cost per trade (when you buy or sell a stock) should be around $10. Some will be more, some less.

For example, I recently saw a television commercial for Scottrade advertising $7 per trade. Since you probably won't be trading that frequently, a few dollars more or less is probably not a big deal. So I tend to choose these things based more on ease of use.

Another consideration is how many trades you may do per year. Your number of trades may range from none to no more than five or ten in some months (and that's kind of high, actually). Note that I said typically here. I may have made forty trades in one month during the peak of the market problems in 2008-2009 – but that is not typical.

Another consideration is whether you work in an office during the day and want to occasionally check on your stocks. In this case you may be accessing your online stockbroker account through your employer's computer. You will want to make sure the broker you chose can be accessed through your companies' computer firewall.

I can tell you from personal experience that TDAmeritrade works fine through the firewalls of companies I've worked for in the past, and I have read that Scottrade is set up this way as well.

The others listed above may very well work too, but you will want to verify this up front with them when you are setting up your stock account.

Opening An Account

To open an account you will need some basic information such as…

Your Social Security Number or Individual Taxpayer Identification Number (ITIN)
Your employer name and address

It should take just a few minutes to fill out the application for a simple, individual account. And it is not complicated if you are making an initial cash deposit to set it up.

It gets a bit more involved if you are opening an IRA account, and transferring stocks and funds from 401k's that you have had with previous employers. If you are doing this, then you will need a copy of you 401k accounts before you start. But don't be put off by this additional paperwork.

This is actually a good idea to consolidate your old 401k's into one account that you can manage. Otherwise, they are just sitting there, going up and down based on the whims of the market. And probably costing you too much in fees, as they are notorious for that. Also, you will have many more investment choices in your new consolidated account.

When I was a broker, I often helped people consolidate all of their old 401k's, which they couldn't do anything with, into a new account. This way they could take control of their future, and trade and direct these funds they had accumulated from past employers.

So if you want to start investing in stocks, take the time to open your broker account. And remember, you only have to do this once. Then you are good to go.

The Online Broker That I Use

I have used TDAmeritrade for much of my personal investing for over eleven years and been very satisfied with them. They are responsive in case I need to call them – which is rare – and I have recommended them to my friends.

To put that in context, when I was a stockbroker, I had my personal account with the national broker dealer I worked for. And as you can image, it had full online capabilities. But once I left the brokerage, I moved my account to TDAmeritrade, which also offered me all of the online capabilities I need.

One final thing to mention here. Outside of having my personal accounts with TDAmeritrade, I have no affiliation with them. And I receive no compensation for mentioning that I use them. I am simply relating to you my personal experience.

So feel free to choose whichever broker you like.

But don't agonize over this. Just choose one and get on with it. This is literally your last step you need to take before you can start buying and selling stocks. So if you just can't make up your mind, you can do what I did and just choose TDAmeritrade.

So get started on opening your account. Because we are getting ready to show you how to buy your first stock.

6

HOW TO BUY AND SELL STOCKS

Once you have your stockbroker account, there are three main things you will do with it. And these are...

> Looking up the price of a stock (and description, research, price history, etc.)
>
> Buying a stock
>
> Selling a stock

That's it. Kind of like you only do three main things with your checking account at the bank. You typically check your balance. And you make deposits and withdrawals. It's about that simple.

So let's get started with how you will look up the price of a stock.

What Is The Price?

So if you were going to buy a new pair of slacks or a dress, you would first go to the store (or online) and find out the price. If the price wasn't too high, you would go ahead and make your purchase.

It's the same way with buying a stock. You need to find out the price and make sure it's not too high before you buy it.

To do this, log in to your stock account web site. Then click on tabs that say something like Research and Ideas —>Stocks. Or, most screens on the site will have a search box that says something like "Symbols or Keywords" that you can type in the stock symbol and press a Search button.

Let's say you want to buy stock in Sprint. If you know that the symbol is S, then enter S in the search box and click the Go button (or Search button).

This will show you a screen similar to the one below.

Or if you don't know the symbol, you can enter "Sprint" in the search box and click on the Symbol Lookup button. This will list all the stocks that have Sprint in their name, and what their symbols are. Pick the symbol for the one that is Sprint, enter it into the search box and click the Go button.

Either way, you will get to a screen that looks something like this:

Figure 6-1. Stock Price Lookup Screen

So what does this tell us?

First, that the full company name of Sprint is Sprint Nextel Corp.

Also that it is a communications services company, and (shown in light grey) that it is traded on the New York Stock Exchange (NYSE).

To the right, it shows a little chart of how the stock has been going up and down over the past months. In this case, it looks like the overall trend is up, but the current price is down.

That's encouraging. It means you could buy it today at a lower price, kind of like it is on sale. And most important, below the Buy and Sell buttons, is the price of $5.17 per share, that you can buy it for right now.

So here's the deal. If your newsletter recommendation said "Buy Sprint (NYSE: S) up to $5.50," should you go ahead and buy the stock?

The answer is yes. The stock, currently at $5.17, is under the highest price of $5.50 that the newsletter recommends you buy it at.

What if your newsletter recommendation said "Buy Sprint (NYSE: S) up to $5.00." Should you go ahead and buy the stock?

The answer is no.

Because the analyst that wrote the recommendation up to $5.00 did a lot of research for you. And they calculated that your best odds of making money with this stock were if you buy it at $5.00 or below. In this case, since you are paying for their research, you would follow their advice and not buy the stock right now.

But for now, let's say the recommendation was up to $5.50. So you are going to buy the stock.

The next thing you will need to do is decide how many shares you are going to buy.

Buying A Stock

Let's say you have about $500 dollars you want to invest in Sprint. Then you can buy about 100 shares, which will cost a total of $517 (100 shares X $5.17 per share). So you decide to buy 100 shares.

When you buy shares of stock, you are actually placing an order into the system. Then that order gets filled and you own the stock. Just like when you go to MacDonald's to buy a hamburger, you place an order. Then the order gets filled, i.e. they hand you the burger and take your money.

So let's place your order for Sprint stock. Since you were just looking at Sprint stock it's still being displayed on your screen. And right there in front of you is a BUY button. So click the BUY button and that will take you to a screen that looks something like this.

Figure 6-2. Buying A Stock Screen

So what does all of that mean?

Well, you see something that says **Bid $5.00**. That's the highest price anyone is willing to pay for the stock at the moment. In other words, people like you, who want to buy Sprint stock, just like you, have said they will pay up to $5.00 a share. They have put in an order at $5.00 a share.

Remember, this is similar to an auction, and $5.00 is the highest bid at the moment. But no one is willing to sell Sprint stock for $5.00.

How do you know this? Because of the other thing you see on the screen, which says **Ask $5.17.** This is the lowest price anyone trying to sell the stock says they will take for it. It's the price they are asking for. So if you try to buy it for less than that, they probably won't sell it to you. Your BUY order will not get filled.

Finally, you see **Last $5.15.** This tells you how much someone sold the stock for in the last transaction, probably in the past few seconds or minutes. So some of the sellers may be weakening on their price. Remember that these prices are constantly changing – that this is an auction going on. The current price "right this minute" is somewhere between $5.17 (ask) and $5.15 (bid).

You are confident this is a fair price because your newsletter recommendation said to buy up to $5.50.

So you are going to place your order for $5.17 because you want to get the stock, and this seems to be a fair price. Here's how you do that.

By the way, there are more advanced ways you can buy that we get into in **More Stock Investing For Beginners**, but right now I just want to walk you through the process in a straightforward manner. And this will work fine for you for now.

But in **More Stock Investing For Beginners** we get into what I call the Warren Buffett mindset. It goes something like this. Just because the stock is selling for $5.17 right now doesn't mean you can't put an order in for $5.00. We get into how to do this and how your odds of making a profit can be much improved.

In the ACTION box, click the drop down so it says Buy. Don't confuse this with the Buy To Open – that is for stock options, which you are not doing. Just select Buy.

Next enter 100 in the Quantity as shown in the illustration. This means you want to buy 100 shares of stock.

Next make sure the ORDER TYPE says limit. This means you don't want to buy it for more than $5.17, i.e. you are limiting the maximum price you will pay for the stock. Then enter the price of $5.17 in the PRICE box. This means you want to buy your shares for $5.17 a share or lower.

And then, in the TIME-IN-FORCE box pick Day. That means you want the order to stay in effect all day until the stock is bought. If the stock does not get bought by the end of the day, then the order is canceled.

Now click the Review button and check the display carefully to make sure the order is correct. It should say something like "Buy 100 shares of S Sprint at $5.17 a share for a total of $517.00."

If the order is not correct, press the Change Order button and make the appropriate changes. Then press the Review Order button one more time to check again. If everything looks okay, press the Place Order button.

Upon pressing the Place Order button, your order goes into the New York Stock Exchange, along with millions of other orders from around the world, and the exchange starts trying to match your buy order to a sell order, so it can buy the stock for you at the price you specified. For most stocks this will only take a few seconds, minutes at the most, and you will see a screen pop up that says your order has been successfully filled.

Now, to confirm that, go back to your Balances and Positions screen and you should see your 100 shares of stock listed there. To get to that screen, click on the Accounts -- > Balances and Positions tabs and scroll down until you see the stock.

Congratulations! You just bought your first shares of stock.

Buying a stock usually happens as simply as described above. But what if the system doesn't come back and say your order was successfully filled? That means it is still looking for a seller that will sell at the price you offered - and it hasn't found one yet.

So you can just wait a while longer to see if it will find a seller for that price. Or you can change your order by raising the price you will pay by a few cents. That will usually get your offer filled.

Similarly, when selling a stock, if your order isn't filled, you can just wait a while longer to see if the system can find a buyer. Or you can lower your asking price by a few cents. And that will usually get your stock sold. We discuss selling in the next chapter.

Selling A Stock

The process of selling your stock is a lot like buying it.

WHEN to sell your stock is a different story. The most sophisticated investors have trouble with this question, including legendary investor Warren Buffett. So don't feel too bad about yourself if you puzzle over this question as well.

That said, here are two times when you would sell your stock.

One time is when you have lost 25% on the stock. We'll get into that in the next section of this book. But for right now, we'll just say you would want to sell in this case, to limit your losses.

The other time to sell is the happier occasion when you have made money, and want to take your profits.

So let's say a few months have gone by and your Sprint stock, which you bought for $5.17 a share, is now going for $10.00 a share.

Wow. Nice profit. So you decide to sell your 100 shares for $10 a share. You bought them for a total of $517. And you are going to sell them for $1000. That's a happy story.

To do this, log in to your stock account and then click on the Accounts -> Balances and Positions tab. This will list all the stocks you own, line by line. Look for the Sprint stock and its symbol, carefully noting how many shares you own (which is 100 in this example).

You can do this by clicking on the stock directly on that screen, or you can click on Research and Ideas -> Stocks tabs and enter the symbol S in the box.

Either way will get you to the screen that shows the current value of the stock. Remember, this is exactly the same screen you went to when you were getting ready to buy the stock.

You will see something like the screen that follows. This screen should look familiar. So what does this tell us?

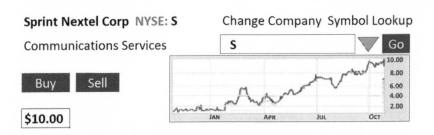

Figure 6-3. Stock Price Lookup Screen

First, that we got the right stock (Sprint). This is the one we want to sell. And second, that the stock's value is now $10.00 a share.

That's all we need to know. So now we click the Sell button. That will bring us to a screen like this one.

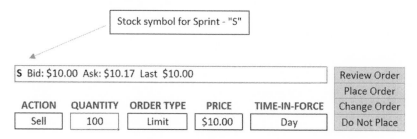

Figure 6-4. Selling A Stock Screen

So what does all of that mean?

Well, you see something that says Bid $10.00. That's the price that people who want to buy the stock are willing to pay for it at this moment.

The next thing you see says Ask $10.17. This is the lowest price anyone that is trying to sell the stock is willing to sell it for at the moment. But you've already decided that $10.00 is the price you are willing to sell for, because you will make a nice profit. So you are going to underbid those $10.17 sellers.

Finally, you see Last at $10.00. This tells you how much someone sold the stock for in the last transaction, probably in the past seconds or minutes. That works out just fine. That's just what you are going to sell for anyway.

You remember that these prices are constantly changing – that this is an auction going on. And that the current price "right this minute" is $10.00. That's the bid price. That's what people are willing to buy the shares you are selling right now. And you are ready to sell your shares for $10.00 a share right now.

So you get ready to sell by filling in the boxes.

Here's how you do that.

Make sure the ACTION BOX says Sell. Do not chose Sell To Close. That is for stock options. Just use Sell.

Enter 100 in the quantity. That's the number of shares you are going to sell.

CAUTION! Make sure you DO NOT accidently enter more shares than you own. Be very careful with this box when you are selling. If you enter more shares than you own, you are trying to do something called "selling short." This can create a big liability for you. By that I mean you could lose much more than your investment. So just be careful with it and don't enter more shares than you own.

There is a time and place to sell short, and we get into that in *More Stock Investing For Beginners*. But it's beyond the scope of this book. And not to be overly dramatic here, but selling short without knowing what you are doing has caused some people to take huge losses, like losing their car, house, etc.

Next make sure the ORDER TYPE says limit. That means you don't want to sell for less than $10.00 a share, i.e. you are limiting the downside on the price.

Then enter the price of $10.00 in the PRICE box. This means you want to sell your shares at $10.00 a share (or better). And then in the TIME-IN-FORCE box pick Day.

This means you want the order to stay in effect all day until the stock sells. If the stock does not sell by the end of the day then the order is canceled.

Now click the Review button and check the display carefully to make sure the order is correct. It should say something like "Sell 100 shares of S Sprint at $10.00 a share for a total of $1000.00."

If the order is not correct, press the Change Order button and make the appropriate changes.

Then press the Review Order button one more time to check again. If everything looks okay, press the Place Order button.

Now your sell order just went out to the New York Stock Exchange, along with millions of other orders, and the exchange is trying to match your sell order to a buy order, so it can sell the stock for you at the price you specified (or better).

For most stocks this will only take a few seconds, minutes at the most, and you will see a screen pop up that says your order has been successfully filled.

Now go back to your Balances and Positions screen and you should see that your 100 shares of stock are no longer listed. You will also see where your cash total just went up by $1000 (less the commission).

Congratulations! You just sold your first shares of stock.

OK, so now you know how to buy and sell stocks. And over time, using recommendations from newsletters and other credible sources, you will begin to own a number of different stocks in your account. This list of stocks you own is called your portfolio.

But now that you own a number of stocks in your portfolio, how do you protect them? How do you keep from having large losses that you hear other people have? And how do you keep your profits?

To learn the answers to these important questions, read on.

7

PROTECTING YOUR STOCK INVESTMENTS

The legendary investor Warren Buffett has two great rules for investing. They are ...

Rule 1: Don't lose the money.
Rule 2: See rule number 1.

This is a huge key to successful investing. So protecting your stock investments is probably the most important thing you will learn in this book. This is how you make money and keep from having big losses. You know, losses like you may have heard other investors have taken, or may have experienced yourself.

Now there are two main things you need to do to protect your portfolio. And both are simple to understand. *So if you just do these two things, you will be way ahead of the average investor.*

One technique is to strictly limit your losses.

The other is to not put all of your eggs in one basket. You've heard that phrase before, right? Meaning that if you drop the basket, all of your eggs break. So we'll start with that one first.

Too Many Eggs In One Basket

This is also known as diversification, and it means you should own a number of different stocks, and never invest all of your money in one single stock. If you do, you are taking unnecessary risk, and could have a big loss.

Why? Because none of us can predict the future. And you never know if there will be a headline tomorrow that says something really bad just happened at that one company that you are invested in.

Like ENRON, for example. There were people that had their entire retirement investment in this one company's stock. Then one day they woke up and there was a bad headline in the news about ENRON. It said the management had been cooking the books and reporting profits that were completely made up.

The stock value dropped, plummeted actually, and lost half of its value in just one week. And by the end of the scandal, and bankruptcy, the stock had dropped from $90.00 to $.61 a share. That's right, sixty-one cents. It was a total wipeout.

So whenever you are tempted to put all your eggs in one basket, you might take a minute to read about the Enron scandal. It's a sobering and cautionary tale for all investors. You can read about it here at https://en.wikipedia.org/wiki/Enron_scandal.

So be sure to invest in more than one stock.

How many stocks should you be invested in? Opinions vary on this. Most range from five to twenty-five different stocks. And I think five is risky, because you still have 20% of your investments concentrated in a single stock.

Of course, you'll probably have just a few stocks when you first start to build your portfolio. So in the beginning, you will not be as diversified as you should be. But work toward diversifying into more different stocks as soon as you can. You should really shoot for having no more than 4-5% of your portfolio in any one stock. So practically speaking, I tend to stay invested in 20 - 25 stocks. That keeps my exposure to any single stock to no more than 4 - 5%.

Similarly, never invest in all of the same kind of stocks. For example, it would not be smart to invest in J. C. Penney's, Macys and Target. Sure, you are invested in more than one stock, but they are all retail department stores.

So what happens to your account when there is a recession and consumers stop shopping? All of your retail department stores stocks go down — all at once.

So invest in different kinds of stocks to stay diversified as well. Which is really not hard to do if you use the steady stream of new stock recommendation ideas we talked about in the chapter How To Find Good Stocks To Buy.

That stream of investment ideas, whether free or paid for newsletters, will help you be sure to stay diversified. And this is a sign of a good stock investor. It's a good way to protect your investments. And it puts you ahead of the average investor.

Note that on Jim Cramer's Mad Money show on CNBC, he has an excellent segment called Am I Diversified? Investors call in and tell him five of their top stocks. Then he quickly evaluates them and tells them if they are diversified. So you might want to watch this part of his show sometime – it's very instructive – and Jim keeps it entertaining.

Let Your Profits Run And Stop Your Losses

The other way we keep our money is that we "stop" our losses. This activity is actually called using "stop losses," so that's a new term for you here.

So how do we do this? After all, we know that sometimes stocks go up, and sometimes stocks go down. And when stocks are going down, that's losing money, right?

So here's what we really mean by that. We mean we want to limit (stop) our losses, and let our gains run as far as possible. If we do that right, our losses will be smaller than our gains. So overall, we will not lose money. Indeed, we should make money over time.

In order to set a stop loss, we actually decide up front, when we buy a stock, how much we are willing to lose before we throw in the towel and sell it.

Making this decision up front is the best time to do this. That's because you have no money on the table yet, so you are more objective. Let me say that another way. When you have bought a stock, i.e. you have money on the table, it's emotional. The idea here is to get the emotions out of the process before buying the stock.

So let's talk about stop losses. A good stop loss percent to use is 25%. This means if you invested $1000 in a stock, and it went down by $250, so it's now only worth $750, you sell it and take the $250 loss.

Why 25% you ask? Well, some credible research and testing against the stock market in the past (known as back testing) has shown that stop losses in the 21% - 27% range have yielded the most efficient results as far as protecting investments.

Setting the stop losses too small, say 10%, caused people to sell their investments too early and too often, only to see them turn around and go higher. And larger stop losses, say 40% to 50%, allowed too much loss before bailing out of a stock in a downward trend.

Sounds simple enough, right? But let me caution you about that. Because this is one of those things that is "simple, but it ain't easy."

Here's why. Because when one of your stocks starts losing money, you will want to hang on to that stock. Back to your $1000 investment in a stock, when it goes down to $750, you will think, well, maybe it will come back up to $1000, and I won't lose any money. Every molecule in your body will be screaming to hang on to that stock, and not take the 25% loss – because you just know it will come back up.

Don't do this. Don't hang on to that stock. Because here's what can happen.

The stock may go on down, to a 35% loss. But hey, you still have hope, so you hang on. Then it's down by 50% -- now you've just got to hang on because you've lost half your money and you want to recover it.

Then it's down 75%, and you are so depressed you don't know what to do. But it keeps going down. Now you're down 90%, so you think, well, I might as well keep it, because I've lost most of my money anyway.

You are correct about part of that. You have lost the money. You broke rule number 1, "Don't lose the money." And rule number 2 also, come to think of it. Looking back on it, you really, really, really wish you had sold that stock when it was only down 25%, right? That 25% loss doesn't look so bad now.

So don't let this happen to you. Be smart, and if your stock goes down 25%, get out while you still have 75% left. Because that will leave you with most of your money to invest in another stock, one that may go up and make you money.

So you will live to invest another day. But if you ride it all the way down to a 90% loss, you are dead in the water. You will have to start all over again.

So those are the basics of stop losses. We show how to do an even smarter kind of stop loss in *More Stock Investing For Beginners*. It's called a trailing stop loss. And it helps you lose even less, and even bail out of a losing stock at a profit some times.

But for this beginning book, we keep it simple with the 25% stop loss. If you can do just this, you are way ahead of most investors.

HOW TO CALCULATE YOUR STOP LOSS: Here's a shortcut you can use to calculate how low your stock can go before you need to sell it, i.e. what your stop loss amount is. Just multiply how much you paid for the stock times .75. If your stock has gone lower than that, it's time to sell.

For example, let's say you bought a stock for $100 a share. Then your stop loss amount is $75 (100 X .75). If your stock is now worth less than $75, you should sell it to keep from losing any more money. Or another example: You bought another stock for $43.95 a share. Your stop loss is $32.96 ($43.95 X .75). So if this stock is now worth less than $32.96, you should sell it.

Or, even easier, your stockbroker account will probably show what percent loss, or gain, you have with each of your stocks. In that case, if the percent loss shows higher than 25% for one of your stocks, then you should sell that stock.

Checking Up On Your Stocks From Time To Time

Once you have begun to invest in stocks and build your portfolio, you will want to check up on them from time to time. Stock investing is not a complete "set it and forget it" proposition, because the value of stocks changes constantly. Remember that they are continuously being bought and sold at the exchanges (auctions) all the time.

That said, there's no need to obsess over them, constantly checking their latest prices, and glued to a stock quote computer screen. This is more of a matter of personal choice and what works best for you.

I typically check up on my stocks a few times a day, and occasionally skip a day here and there. That's what works for me. But that may be too frequent for you. Maybe you prefer to check up on your stocks every day or so, or a couple of times a week. I even know of a Palm Beach multimillionaire who only checks his portfolio once a week. So that's a pretty wide range you can fit in.

The one exception to this is when the stock market is dropping over a period of days. Or you have a stock that has almost lost 25% in value, i.e. it's about to hit its stop loss limit. Now you are on alert to be ready to sell and cut your losses.

In this case, at a minimum, you should check up on that stock at the end of every day after the market has closed. Then, if you see the closing price of your stock has dropped below your 25% stop loss limit, you should plan to sell it the next day.

An easy way to check out your stocks is to just log in to your stock account, which is constantly updated. It will show you a list of all your stocks (your portfolio) and what they are worth at that point in time. It will also show you their individual gains or losses.

FUN BUT NOT NECESSARY: Sometimes after I've checked on my stocks, I wait a minute and hit the refresh key again. This will show how their value has changed in that short period of time, as buyers and sellers around the world bought and sold in the past 60 seconds.

It's kind of fun, and interesting, as you watch the world of finance in action, real time. But this is certainly not necessary, and you probably have better things to do with your time. Come to think of it, I probably do to.

Another place I go to look up stocks is on Yahoo. I even used Yahoo sometimes when I was a stockbroker, if I was looking up a stock we didn't have listed. To look up a stock on Yahoo, just go to www.Yahoo.com. Click the Finance section on the left of the screen. Then enter the stock symbol at the top and hit the return key.

Your stock and its current price will appear. Additionally, you can see a chart of how it has been doing over the past days, weeks, years, etc., by clicking on various time frames.

I also go to Yahoo to look at some of the comments other owners have made in the message board. You can see these by clicking the message board link on the left. Many of the comments are quite interesting. Some are informative, and others rather trivial.

All that said, you usually don't need to check on your stocks all that frequently. And many stock account sites allow you to set up email alerts that will trigger if a stock is dropping below your stop loss limit. This can be very handy and useful.

And finally, the real key to success is to buy good stocks at good prices. Because over time, even as their value goes up and down, they should trend upward over time.

8

ADDITIONAL RESOURCES

At this point, you've learned all the basics you need to start investing in stocks.

I've given you the exact steps to use to get started. Essentially, these are the same steps I wound up using many years ago. I say "essentially," because my path was not so simple and direct. And that's because I didn't have a book like this to get started.

But it's the same basic system I would use to get started today.

With that said, we covered a number of resources in this book. So this section lists them all for you as a handy reference. And some additional resources as well.

NOTE that print book readers can access this chapter and the live links at <u>www.LiveLearnAndProsper.com/ar.</u>

More Stock Ideas at the Live Learn and Prosper Web Site
http://www.LiveLearnAndProsper.com/
Learn more valuable information about stock investing at my web site. Learn more profitable techniques, get sample chapters from upcoming books, and learn about other types of investments. And much, much more.

Free Newsletter
http://www.LiveLearnAndProsper.com/n
Get even more valuable stock ideas to build your wealth in our monthly Live Learn And Prosper Newsletter. You can sign up here for FREE. And no, this is not a free trial where we try to get you to pay after fourteen days like the other sites. This is free. We will not ask for your credit card.

100 Year Historical Charts
http://www.macrotrends.net
A great source for historical trends of the stock market by Macrotrends. They go back 100 years, and show interesting breakouts, such as by President, by Fed Chairman and by Recession.

List Of Stock Symbols
https://en.wikipedia.org/wiki/List_of_S%26P_500_companies
A handy list of the stock symbols for the top 500 companies in the United States, known as the S&P 500. S&P stands for Standard & Poor's, an organization that has been providing financial market information for more than 150 years.

Free Stock Recommendations – Mad Money - Jim Cramer
https://www.thestreet.com/mad-money
A web site that publishes Jim Cramer's stock recommendations from his nightly television show on CNBC called Mad Money.

Free Stock Recommendations – Fast Money - Melissa Lee
http://www.cnbc.com/fast-money
A web site that publishes stock recommendations from Melissa Lee's Fast Money on CNBC. Alternatively, just Google "Fast Money Final Trade" to see their latest recommendations.

Paid Stock Recommendations - The Oxford Club – For Growth Stocks Recommendations
https://oxfordclub.com/communique
An excellent, affordable stock investing newsletter. I have used Oxford Club for years.

Paid Stock Recommendations - The Oxford Club – For Income Stocks Recommendations
https://oxfordclub.com/income-letter/
An excellent, affordable stock investing newsletter. I have used Oxford Club for years.

Discount Broker Web Sites
    TDAmeritrade - www.tdameritrade.com
    Scottrade - www.scottrade.com

E*Trade - www.etrade.com
Fidelity Investments - www.fidelity.com
Charles Schwab - www.schwab.com
I've used TDAmeritrade for years.

Free Stock Information and Charts
https://finance.yahoo.com/
Yahoo Finance is a useful site for stock market news and to research specific stocks. Just enter the stock symbol at the top of the screen and click the Search Finance button.

Tracking Your Stop Losses
https://tradestops.com/
Very useful if you have many different stock positions and want to use sophisticated stop loss tracking. I use it, but note that it is a paid for subscription service. However, it's not necessary for beginners with a few stock positions. You can probably use your discount brokers free alert system instead.

Conclusion

You've gained a lot of valuable information at this point.

To recap, you've learned:

• That most of the top ten percent, the wealthy, are business owners.

• And owning stocks is one of the easiest ways to become a business owner.

• *So stock investing can increase your wealth - like the top ten percent increase their wealth.*

• Stock investing is easier and cheaper than ever before.

• And there are newsletters and other sources that can give you winning stock ideas.

• So you don't need to do any complicated analysis.

• You also learned how to open a stock investment account.

• And how to find and buy your first winning stock.

• And how to protect your stock investments.

• *So you know everything you need to know to get started.*

Now it's up to you to use this information and start on your path to wealth by investing in stocks.

Don't waste time and regret thinking you should have done this a long time ago. Just remind yourself of the old adage that says, "The best time to plant a tree is 20 years ago; the second-best time is now."

There's no time like the present, so why not get started and immediately apply what you've learned. Don't just close this book and move on to something else.

Instead, gather your information to open a stock account. And then call a broker and open your account. Then, using newsletters or the TV shows we mentioned, make a commitment to find your first great stock to invest in. Take a few days to decide. Then go out to your account and buy your first stock.

Now you are on your way. You're sitting at the other side of the table, where the wealthy people sit. That's the side where other people work hard to increase YOUR wealth. Just like the top ten percent do.

Because now you are a business owner. And you have started down the path to a more secure financial future.

I wish you the very best of success on your road to prosperity as a new stock investor!

John

http://www.LiveLearnAndProsper.com

Would You Like To Know More

Understanding and using the basics of stock investing you just learned puts you way ahead of most investors. You now have the basic skills to invest in any of the 8000 stocks listed on the exchanges.

But there is an amazing group of those stocks, about 1400 of them, **that can grow your wealth AND pay you income too.** This is not some theoretical concept we are talking about here. I'm talking about real checks coming to you in the mail, every 30 to 90 days.

You could, in fact, get your first check in your mailbox in 30-90 days once you know about these stocks. And they keep paying you, month after month, quarter after quarter.

We actually touched on this subject in the book when we mentioned dividend paying stocks. But there is much, much more for you to know about this fascinating class of stocks.

Like how you can think of their dividends as paychecks. And by investing in them over time, you start building your future paychecks. Just think about that for a minute. You can start building your future paychecks for retirement, or supplement your current income. Starting now.

But it gets better yet, because many of these stocks also increase their payout to you every year. That's like getting raises. And I'm not talking trivial little raises of 1 or 2 percent like you get at work - if you get a raise at all. Some of these stocks raise their payout by as much as 10 percent.

In my title, <u>Your Future Paychecks And Raises - Get Dividend Checks In Your Mailbox Paid To The Order Of YOU!,</u> I give the exact techniques and blueprint you can use to…

Find these special dividend paying stocks.

Identify which ones are best to maximize your checks and profit.

Compound your wealth…. how to turbocharge them with a powerful re-investment technique.

And many more tricks and tips to increase your wealth.

You have the skills to do this now. All you need to do is learn about these special, dividend paying stocks. So if you want to take your investment success to the next level, and get paid in the process, then this book is for you.

Just click here to learn more about <u>Your Future Paychecks And Raises - Get Dividend Checks In Your Mailbox Paid To The Order Of YOU!</u>

More Books By John

<u>Stock Investing For Beginners - How To Buy Your First Stock And Grow Your Money</u>

The upper ten percent use stocks to grow their income and wealth. Here's just what you need to get started and join the club. You will be able to buy your first stock by the end of this book. Available in eBook format.

<u>Stock Market For Beginners - Simple Steps To Get Started And Achieve Your Goals</u>

If you liked *Stock Investing For Beginners*, this is a large, easy to read paperback with additional chapters covering many more useful topics. Similar to *Stock Investing For Beginners*, it covers how most wealthy people are business owners. And it reveals how stocks are the easiest way for you to become a business owner and increase your wealth. By the end of the book you will be able to buy your first stock.

Your Future Paychecks And Raises - Get Dividend Checks In Your Mailbox Paid To The Order Of YOU!

Investing in dividend stocks is one of the most profitable ways to invest. That's because YOU GET PAID while you invest. They will actually send you checks in the mail. And you don't have to wait a long time, either. You can get your first check in 30 - 90 days. Learn how to get these checks, and how they allow you to build your future paychecks and raises too. You will learn where to find these profitable stocks, how to invest in them, and start getting your first checks – PAID TO THE ORDER OF YOU.

Future Books and FREE First Chapters

Be sure and check out these future books by John. You can also get the first chapters for free as they become available.

Silver Investing For Beginners - Invest In REAL Money Today For A Wealthier Future Tomorrow

The dollar has lost over 40% of its value in the last ten years. But silver has served as honest money for mankind for thousands of years. Learn how investing in silver today can increase your future wealth while the dollar continues to drop. And you can invest for just $3 to begin. Even a child can use the $3 technique - and some do. Soon to be available in eBook format.

Stock Options for Beginners - Invest Less Money And Make Bigger Profits With Options

It's possible to make 50%, 100% and more in a few weeks or months with stock options, while investing and risking less money. Learn how to add this valuable investing technique to your skill set. Soon to be available in eBook format.

More Stock Investing For Beginners - Pro Techniques To Turbocharge Your Wealth

The professionals have a number of tricks they use to increase their stock investing odds for profits. You can learn them here and use them too.

More Stock Options For Beginners - Winning Strategies Of The Pros

The professionals use many different strategies to win with stock options. Imagine being able to make an investment and profit from it, even if it goes up, down, or stays the same. Learn how the pros put the odds in their favor like this.

Make More Money With Special Stock-Like Investments

There are many other types of stock-based and partnership investments you can profit from. And they are as easy to invest in as stocks. For example, there are certain special stock-like investments where you must be paid 90% of the profits by law, and the company pays no taxes on the profits. And many more to boost your investment profits.

Thank You

Before you go I'd like to say "thank you" for purchasing my eBook. I know you could have picked from hundreds of books on Kindle publishing. But you took a chance with my book.

So a big thank you for downloading it and reading it all the way to the end.

If you liked this book, then I could use your help. Could you please take a moment to leave a review of this book on Amazon.

Your important opinion and feedback will help me continue to write the type of Kindle books that help you get results. And if you really liked it, please let me know at JohnRoberts@LiveLearnAndProsper.com.

ABOUT THE AUTHOR

JOHN ROBERTS is the Founder and CEO of Live Learn And Prosper.com, a newsletter and website focused on getting the most out of investments and life. His books and articles are known for their easy to understand writing style explaining complex things.

He's been a life-long investor and was a former licensed Stockbroker, Financial Consultant and Senior Business Analyst. Prior to that, he managed the Corporate IT Department of a Fortune 500 Corporation. And yet earlier, served as the Senior Programmer/Designer for May Department Stores International, spending time in London, England designing and programming a large scale international foreign buying system. He also served in the United States Marine Corps.

But all is not work and investments in John's life. Called a renaissance man by his friends, he is also an award winning photographer, cartoonist, published author and avid sailor, believing that life should be an adventure.

He recalls one Thanksgiving finding himself singlehandedly sailing his boat the *Saline Solution* in the Florida Keys — on the far edge of tropical storm Keith. He says when he finally made it back safely to port, it was the most thankful Thanksgiving of his life. He also allows this may have been a bit too much adventure.

John's had a life-long commitment to self-improvement and achieving goals. He had an early start with higher goals as a "lettered" fiberglass pole-vaulter in high school, clearing 12' when the world record was 17'.

John currently resides in Orlando. Florida. When he's not busy writing you can often find him soaking up sun at the beach.

Made in the USA
Columbia, SC
11 February 2020